Dave Marsh

[The Great Rock 'n' Roll joke Book]

Kathi Kamen Goldmark

Introduction by Roy Blount, jr.

Illustrations by Gretchen Shields

ST. MARTIN'S GRIFFIN

NEW YORK

Design by Songhee Kim

Library of Congress Cataloging-in-Publication Data

Marsh, Dave.
    The great rock 'n' roll joke book / Dave Marsh and Kathi Kamen Goldmark.
       p. cm.
    ISBN 0-312-16859-4
    1. Rock music—Humor. I. Goldmark, Kathi Kamen.
II. Title.
PN6231.R59M37   1997
818'.5402—dc21   97-19549
                                       CIP

First St. Martin's Griffin Edition: October 1997

10 9 8 7 6 5 4 3 2 1

[The Great Rock 'n' Roll Joke Book]

Dedicated in loving merriment to

Jessica Mitford,

who taught us

what to say about people who can't take a joke

[Acknowledgments]

Kathi thanks:

Dave for saying "Hey! This could be a book!"; Gretchen for the cool illustrations; Roy for the swell intro; Sandy Choron for selling it; and Jim Fitzgerald for buying it. Joe and Tony Goldmark, Audrey de-Chadenèdes and David O. Golia, for putting up with me; Daniel Berman, Keta Bill, Mike Billo, Paul Kamen, Stephen King, Michael Ross, Joel Selvin, and Peter Tucker for keeping those jokes coming; Lorraine Battle, bandmates Kathleen, Chris, David, Henry and The Rock Bottom Remainders, for listening to 'em; Gail Parenteau and George Gerrity

for everything; and every drummer
I ever met.

        Dave thanks:

Kathi, Tony, Barbara, and the le-
gions of poor citizens who have put
up with my bad jokes for years, es-
pecially James and David Dunning,
Kathy Hammer, Sasha Carr, and
Roy Blount. Fuck everybody else.

[contents]

[Contents]

[Contents]   xi

xii [Contents]

[Introduction]

A while back I met a friend of Dave Marsh's. She said, "I hear you're in a rock 'n' roll band together."

"That's right," I said. "We have sung side by side in ten cities. And Dave is *terrible*."

She looked taken aback, so I assured her hastily that *terrible* was hip musicians' talk for, like, *incandescent*. In fact, I meant *terrible*.

But fraternally. I meant it sort of in the spirit of a "Far Side" cartoon I saw once. A boy dog is at a girl dog's door holding a bouquet, he's there to pick her up for a date, she's blushing prettily, and he's saying by way of sincere appreciation, "I don't know what you rolled in, but it sure does stink!"

Sort of in that spirit, but not exactly. Maybe you'd have to have been there, on stage harmonizing just as blood-curdlingly as Dave and I did together (on "Louie, Louie," the FBI-version lyrics; on "Double Shot of My Baby's Love," the never-quite-got-them-memorized lyrics; on "Gloria," the title, including the spelling part to understand . . .)

It's sort of like, if a shortstop is batting .143,

a soft .143, and yet he's playing regularly in big-league parks, he *must* be a hell of a fielder. If someone is part of a rock 'n' roll band that travels in Aretha's former bus and he sings as badly as Dave (modesty prevents me from adding, "or I"), then that someone must have certain *extraordinary* rock 'n' roll virtues, apart from the musical. That someone must be far more nearly on-key than he sounds.

That someone is Dave. At criticizing rock 'n' roll, at explicating rock 'n' roll, at getting red in the face arguing about obscure points of rock 'n' roll—and now, herewith, at collecting state-of-the-art, cutting-edge rock 'n' roll jokes—he is an idol, he is a god, he *is* The Music.

He and Kathi Goldmark. Kathi would appear to be a different kettle of fish. Kathi actually can sing. She actually can play the guitar. She actually looks hot in, like, hot outfits. (Whereas Dave looks like a kettle of fish.) She plays and sings *for money*. Not a lot of money, I guess, but . . . the best way I can say it is this: When Kathi is putting across a song on stage, her microphone—and this is a dream of mine, but no more than just that, a dream—her microphone is actually on.

On the other hand, she is the person who organized the band that Dave and I sang in.

You have to wonder.

Maybe Kathi thought our band of performing authors, The Rock Bottom Remainders (whose other eminent members would surely not go unmentioned here, if they had been roped into writing this introduction) was a rock 'n' roll joke.

Were we a joke? Was I up there singing my heart out—or, if you will, my esophagus—just so a few thousand screaming fans all up and down the Eastern seaboard and Los Angeles could have a laugh at Dave's expense?

I'll tell you this. When you've been a rock star as long as I have, you realize, above all else, one thing: It's not about me. It's not about you, unless your name is Bony Moronie. (Which I doubt.) It's about the music. And that's what Kathi is about. That's what Dave is about. That's what Bruce is about. (Did I mention that Bruce—no, not Kathi's cousin Bruce—Bruce joined us in L.A. on "Gloria"? He is a friend, as we know, of the disadvantaged.)

That's what this book is about. That's what this introduction is about.

And yet I never had a lesson in my life.

I'll tell you something else: *I do not, myself, get all of these jokes.* That is to say: I get all of some of them, but only parts of others. See, these are not jokes that circulate among people who, like, "love music." These are jokes that circulate among people who make music. People who, for instance, actually know what the role of a drummer is, i.e., to hang out with musicians.

I will now give you my personal guarantee: If you spend just ten minutes a day mastering the jokes in this book, you, too, can hang out with musicians. Assuming you'll sign for the room service, take the rap if someone gets killed, and there's no place you absolutely have to be before three o'clock the next afternoon. Make that four-thirty. Six, to be safe. And you're loose enough that it's not going to be this big trauma or something if you have to go to jail naked.

I just wish I had known all these jokes—whether I got them or not—when I was hanging out with musicians. Simulated musicians. Well, Kathi was a real one. Certainly she had the best brea . . . th control (to all outward appearances) in the band. Amy's stood out, too (we had a chick singer named Amy, whom I don't notice taking any part in writing this introduction), but the bulk of hers was simulated. Dave's looked like a kettle of fish.

Ahh, well, Lordy Lordy. You had to be there.

In closing, let's see . . . Wanna bet I can't make up a rock 'n' roll joke from scratch?

What did James Brown say when he got out of jail and found that his uproarious in-jokes about life behind bars elicited nothing but blank stares on the outside?

He said, "Ahh, well . . ." or, no: "*Good God!* You had to be there."

—Roy Blount, Jr.

[The Great Rock 'n' Roll Joke Book]

How many guitar players does it take to change a light bulb?

Ten. One to change the bulb, nine to sit around and say, "I can do that better."

What does a lead guitar player use for contraception?

His personality.

Why don't guitar players get mad cow disease?

They're all pigs.

Why do medical labs prefer guitarists to rats?

Because they're cheaper, breed faster, and there are some things rats just won't do.

How do you get a guitarist to stop playing?

Put sheet music in front of him.

His guitar playing reminds me of Hendrix—they were both left-handed and the new guy makes you *wish* he'd burn it.

What's the best thing to play on a guitar?
  Solitaire.

[String 'Em Up]

Why is an electric guitar like a vacuum cleaner?
   When you turn them on, they both suck.

What do you call a guitar player who just had a fight with his girlfriend?
   Homeless.

Did you hear about the guitar tuners' beauty contest?
   The winner came in third.

Why can't a guitar player make Kool Aid?
   He can't figure out how to fit two quarts of water into that little package.

The guitarist came back from the Milli Vanilli tour looking exhausted. "Jesus! What happened to you?" asked his pals.
   "The tapes broke and we had to play!"

Why do guitarists have the biggest balls?
   Because they send out the most invitations.

For most guitarists, being in a band is like taking a bath—at first, it feels just right, but then it's not so hot.

What's the difference between a guitarist and a mutual fund?
   The mutual fund will eventually mature and start making money.

[String 'Em Up]   3

How many guitar players does it take to change a light bulb?

None. They just steal someone else's light.

[String 'Em Up]

2
[stop that banging!]
Jokes about Drummers

Why does a drummer leave his drumsticks on the dashboard?
So he can park in the handicapped zone.

What has three legs and a dick?
A drum stool.

Why does every band need a bass player?
To translate for the drummer.

A woman walks into a butcher shop to purchase her family's dinner. She spots something that looks interesting, and asks the butcher what it might be.
"Well, ma'am, those are calf brains. They cost $1.50 a pound."
"Oh, okay. What's that, over there?"
"Sheep brains, ma'am. They're $1.75 a pound."
"One more question. What's *that?*"

"Those there, ma'am? Why, those are drummers' brains. And they're $45.50 a pound."

"That's outrageous," exclaims the housewife. "Why does it cost so much for drummers' brains?"

"Well, ma'am, do you have any idea how many drummers' brains it takes to make up a pound?"

How many drummers does it take to change a light bulb?

None. They have these great machines out now that can do *anything* a drummer can do.

What's smarter than two drummers?

One drummer.

What did the drummer say to the chick singer?

"Would you like me to play the next song too fast or too slow?"

There were these two troopers at Fort Apache. They were the only two left alive, because all the rest had been massacred by the Indians. Late that night, they crawled up to look over the wall. Spread out on the plain before them were hundreds, maybe thousands, of Indian campfires, surrounding the fort in every direction. The troops sank back to the ground in despair, knowing that as soon as morning came, they would be goners.

It began to get gray in the East, when all of a sudden, off in the distance, they heard "BOOM boom boom boom BOOM boom boom boom

[Stop That Banging!]

BOOM boom boom boom." One of the troopers looked at the other and said, "I don't like the sound of those drums. . . ."

From off in the distance came a voice: "He's not our regular drummer!"

What does it say on the seat of a drummer's stool?
   "This side up."

What do you call guys who hang out with musicians?
   Drummers.

How do you get a drummer off your doorstep?
   Pay for the pizza.

The band took a week off and the drummer and bass player took off into the wilderness on a backpacking expedition. After a few days, they started to get on each others' nerves, so they decided they'd spend the day hiking in opposite directions. At dusk, each returned to the campsite.

   "Shit," said the bassist. "I had a *really* terrible day. First, I got lost, then I got sunburned, then I tripped over a log and sprained my ankle, then I got bitten by about a million mosquitoes. How'd you do?"

   "I hate to tell you this," said the drummer, "but it was *great*. I went over that hill and discovered a beautiful naked woman tied to an abandoned railroad track. Naturally, I untied her and then we had sex every possible way you could imagine, all afternoon."

"Wow! Did she even give you a blow job?"

"Nope," said the drummer. "I never *did* find her head. . . ."

How can you tell when a drummer is knocking at your door?

The knocks keep getting faster and faster and louder and louder.

How can you tell when the stage is level?

The drool is coming out both sides of the drummer's mouth.

What has five arms, six legs, and eats pussy?

The Indigo Girls and Def Leppard's drummer.

What did the drummer say when he was asked to be a Jehovah's Witness?

"Sorry. I never saw the accident."

What's the difference between a drummer and a pig?

A pig won't stay up all night trying to fuck a drummer.

What do you call a drummer with half a brain?

Gifted.

Why are set breaks limited to twenty minutes?

So you don't have to retrain the drummer.

[Stop That Banging!]

Stevie Ray Vaughan died and went, of course, to hell. When he got there, though, he was delighted to find himself in a rehearsal room with some of his favorite musicians: Berry Oakley of the Allman Brothers on bass, Jimi Hendrix on guitar, Pigpen on piano, Buddy Holly on vocals. He couldn't have been more delighted, even though the stool behind the drum kit remained empty.

So Stevie went over to Oakley and said, "Hey! I can't believe this is hell. I mean, this is the greatest bunch of musicians I ever played with my life. If this *is* hell, what's the catch?"

Just then the door opened and in walked Karen Carpenter, carrying a pair of sticks. "Okay, guys," she said, "One . . . two . . . three . . . 'Why do stars suddenly appear . . . ' "

Why is an orgasm like a drum solo?

You know it's coming and there's nothing you can do to stop it.

A bass player showed up at his manager's office with his hand in a cast. "What happened?" asked the horrified receptionist.

"Well, we were going out to the gig last night and we stopped to get something to eat and when we came back out, I realized that the keys were locked in the car."

"So you had to break the window to get them out?"

"No, I broke my hand pounding on the door, trying to get our drummer's attention."

"I'm not going to say what I asked Santa to get me for Christmas, but my kid's goddamn drum kit is sitting right beneath the chimney."

Did you hear about the confused drummer?

He kept asking for the time and people kept giving him different answers.

  [Stop That Banging!]

"The Bible says, 'Love thy neighbor.'"

"God's next-door neighbor didn't play drums."

The teacher told her class to make a list of the five greatest living humans. After twenty minutes, only one kid still struggled to complete his assignment. The teacher went over to him and asked, "What seems to be the trouble?" The kid looked up and said, "I dunno. Who do *you* think the drummer should be?"

Why do Catholics make the best drummers?

They already practice the rhythm method.

Six guys are sitting at the bar in the neighborhood pub, when the conversation turns to the subject of IQ. The first two guys discover their IQ scores are around 180, and start discussing astrophysics and the theory of relativity. The second two guys compare notes, discover they both have IQ scores around 120, and begin discussing their favorite books, films, and CDs.

Still left out, guy number five turns to his buddy and asks, "So what's your IQ?"

"Oh, around seventy-five."

"Hey! Me, too. What kinda sticks do you use?"

How late does a band usually play?

About two beats behind the drummer.

• • •

[Stop That Banging!]

Why did the chicken cross the road?
   To get away from the drum solo.

What's the most important thing about being a drummTiming.

 [Stop That Banging!]

[A Few That Really Sink to the Bottom]

3

Jokes about Bass Players

How many bass players does it take to change a light bulb?

None. The piano player can do that with her left hand.

A guy goes on vacation to a tropical paradise. He's having a wonderful, totally hedonistic good time, but keeps hearing drums in the background. He repeatedly asks his island hosts why the drums never stop. Every time, they just shake their heads and reply, "Drums stop—very bad."

Finally, after several blissful days, the drums *do* stop. Suddenly, natives are running all over the island, hands held to their ears, panic written on their faces. The tourist finally gets one to slow down long enough to ask, "What the hell is going on?"

The guy keeps running but he shouts back over his shoulder: "Drums stop. Here comes bass solo!"

• • •

What's the range of a fretless bass?
    Twenty yards if you have a good arm.

What did the bass player get on his IQ test?
    Drool.

What's the difference between a bass and a guitar?
    The bass takes longer to burn.

If you were lost in the woods, who would be the best person to give you directions: an out-of-tune bass player, an in-tune bass player, or Santa Claus?
    The out-of-tune bass player. The other two are just signs that you're hallucinating.

During the big California earthquake, which happened just before dawn, a huge temblor rolled through one of the city's biggest discos. "More bass!" yelled the dancers.

Why did the bassist lose his day job at the M&M factory?
    He kept tossing out the Ws.

The hot new band was rehearsing its showcase set, and they sounded great.
    "Wow!" the guitarist thought to himself. "This is the best band I've ever played in! We've got a hit song here. I'm sure we're gonna get a record deal. My financial worries will be history!"
    "Hey!" thought the drummer. "This is *amazing!* We're gonna be famous. Women will be chas-

ing after us. I'll have all the pussy I could ever want."

"Man!" mused the lead singer. "We're gonna be so famous I'll never have to pay for drugs again. The fans'll just hand 'em out."

Meanwhile the bass player was thinking: "E . . . B . . . E . . . B . . . E . . . B . . . E . . . B . . ."

What do you call a bass player's index finger?
His handkerchief.

How come they don't invent a machine to play bass like the ones they have to play drums?
Because it's really hard to get a machine to chew gum and look bored at the same time.

How many bass players does it take to change a light bulb?
None. They can't get up that high.

4

[Crazy 88s]

Jokes about Keyboard Players

What's the difference between a keyboard and a coffin?

The coffin has the corpse *inside.*

How many keyboard players does it take to change a light bulb?

Five. One to handle the bulb, and the other four to contemplate how Rick Wakeman would have done it.

How many jazz pianists does it take to change a light bulb?

Screw the changes, we'll fake it.

Another Grateful Dead piano player died—about their thirtieth—and they had to hire a replacement too quickly to audition him. He turned out to be really terrible—so bad even Deadheads could tell. During a very quiet passage, one guy stood up in the balcony and yelled out that the pianist was a jerk.

"Who called our piano player a jerk?" demanded Bob Weir.

"Who called that jerk a piano player?" yelled the Deadhead.

"I hear that piano player you've been dating has wonderful manners."

"Oh yes—last night at dinner I dropped my purse and he kicked it right back to me."

Then there was the Martian who wandered into a piano store. "Nice teeth," he said. "Who's your dentist?"

"I know you guys just can't wait 'til I die," said the egomaniacal synth player, "so you can spit on my grave."

"Not me," said his personal roadie. "You're crazy if you think I'm gonna wait in a line *that* long."

A piano player went to his girl's father and asked for her hand in marriage. Despite this rather courtly and well-mannered approach to the situation, the father flew into a rage. "Never! Never! I would never allow any of my children to marry a piano player—much less my only daughter, the love of my life!"

"Gee, you know, you haven't even seen me play. Will you at least come and hear our band on Friday night?"

The father at first refused but his daughter pleaded for the next several days, and so on Friday evening, he got in the car and went to the joint where the would-be fiancé's band was appearing. He sat grimly through the show, and as the house lights came up, turned to his daughter and said, "Okay, you can marry him. He's no piano player."

How can you tell if there's a synthesizer player at your door?

You think you hear him knocking, but you're not quite sure.

Did you hear about the vibes player who sold over a million records?

He had a twenty-year career as a clerk at Tower.

"Hey, I use a limo wherever I go," boasted the piano player. "Really?" asked the guitarist. "How long have you been a chauffeur?"

5
[My Kingdom for a Mute!]
Jokes about Horn Players

How do you get two horn players to play in perfect unison?

Shoot one.

What's the difference between a dead snake in the road and a dead trombone player in the road?

The snake might have been on its way to a gig.

Define "optimist."

A trombone player with a beeper.

What does a trombone player say at his gig?

"Hey, you want fries with that?"

Late one night, you enter a jazz club. Sitting at the bar are Saddam Hussein and Adolf Hitler. Unfortunately, since you've just been to a meeting at the record label, there's only one bullet left in your revolver. Who do you shoot?

Kenny G.

What's the difference between a lawn mower and a tuba?

The neighbors would like you to return the lawn mower.

The trombone player won $25 million in the lottery. "Wow! What are you gonna do with all that?" asked his friend, the banjo player.

"I guess I'll keep gigging till the money runs out."

Why don't sax players like playing soprano?

There's no place to hide their drugs.

How many trumpet players does it take to pave a driveway?

About a dozen, if you smooth 'em out right.

The guitar player ran into his high school friend, the trombonist, on a busy street corner. "Hey, how's work?" asked the guitar god.

"Well, I had a gig at the biggest club in town," the trombonist reported with a hangdog look. "But then they put in paper towels."

What's the difference between a tenor sax and O. J. Simpson's story?

The sax has more leaks.

How do you get the horn section to start complaining?

Get 'em a gig.

A trombonist goes to the doctor and complains, "I can't go to the bathroom."

"Okay, take two of these every day and you'll be fine."

Two weeks later he returns. "I still can't go to the bathroom." The doctor doubles the dose. The musician returns in another week, looking terrible, and says, "I still can't go to the bathroom."

"Hmmm," says the doctor, "what did you say you did for a living?"

"I play trombone."

"Oh," said the doctor. "Here's twenty bucks. Try getting yourself something to eat."

Why are horns the most divine instruments?

Because no matter who blows into them, God only knows what's going to come out.

What do you call a guy who can play the trombone but doesn't?

A gentleman.

Entering the music store, the musician said, "I'd like a mute for my trumpet."

"Sounds like a fair trade to me," the sales clerk instantly replied.

•   •   •

[My Kingdom for a Mute!]   21 👄

How can you spot a trombonist's kid on the playground?

He can't swing, and he complains about the slide.

6

[They Do So Play Those in Rock Groups]

Jokes about Banjos, Fiddles, Accordions, and Other Instruments of Torture

What's the difference between an accordion and a trampoline?

You take off your shoes when you jump on a trampoline.

What's the difference between a banjo and an onion?

No one cries when you slice up a banjo.

What's the definition of perfect pitch?

Throwing the banjo into the toilet without hitting the rim.

How can you tell one fiddle tune from another?

By the title.

•   •   •

What's the biggest mistake a musician can make?

Joining an all-girl band as an accordion player.

What's the least-used sentence in the English language?

"Is that the banjo player's Porsche?"

What's the difference between a harmonica and a Harley-Davidson?

You can tune the Harley-Davidson.

Two fathers met on the street. The first bragged boldly about his son, an executive in a major accounting firm. The other father said. "Well, my son is a virtuoso accordion player. He's been acclaimed since childhood. And he just got his first gig."

"Really. How long has he been out of school?"

"Twenty years."

Why do people take an instant dislike to harmonica players?

It saves time.

What's the difference between a banjo and a chain saw?

A chain saw has greater dynamic range.

What do you throw a drowning pedal steel player?

His other amplifier.

The bandleader was about to count off the night's first tune when he noticed the fiddle player glaring at the pedal steel player *again*.

"What's the problem?" he groaned.

"He loosened my tuning peg," whined the fiddler.

"So tighten it!"

"I can't tell which one!"

How many bluegrass musicians does it take to change a light bulb?

Ten. One to change the bulb, and nine to stand around bitching about its being electric.

What's the difference between a harmonica solo and brain surgery?

You get an anesthetic for brain surgery.

Why do banjo players like family reunions?

Great place to meet women.

How many country bass players does it take to change a light bulb?

One, five, one, five, one, five, one, five. . . .

Did you hear about the fiddle player who was so out of tune, even the banjo player noticed?

Three fathers unexpectedly met in the Amazonian jungles of Brazil. The first explained that he had come because, as a petroleum geologist, he wanted to find out if the formations in the area held any promise of an oil strike. The second said that, as a biochemist, he hoped to locate some of the plants that indigenous tribes used to fight infections and cure disease. The third, a florist, remained silent.

"So, Bill," said the geologist, "I guess you're here to track down some rare orchids or something, right?"

"No," said Bill. "I'm here because my son is studying the banjo."

What do you call five thousand harmonicas on the bottom of the ocean?

A damn good start.

Define "genius."

Anybody who can define how an accordion works without using his hands.

What has sixteen arms, sixteen legs, and eight teeth?

The front row of a banjo workshop.

What did they say when the harmonica player fell out of the plane with no parachute?

Who the fuck cares?

7

[Shaddapa You Face]

Jokes about Singers

How many chick singers does it take to change a light bulb?

One. She holds the bulb up to the socket, and waits for the world to revolve around her.

How many feminist folk singers does it take to change a light bulb?

One. *And it's not funny!*

How can you tell when a chick singer is knocking at your door?

She doesn't know when to come in, and she can't find the key.

Why did the punk rock singer cross the road?

He was stapled to a chicken.

· · ·

The blue-eyed soul singer went to James Brown's doctor, complaining that his knees were killing

[Shaddapa You Face]

him. The doc had him take down his pants, and inspected the knees.

"Man, you've got *bone splinters*," exclaimed the doc. "What the hell have you been doing to yourself?"

"I've just been doing that knee drop, just like James Brown," said the singer.

"Well, I think you'd better give it up," said the doctor. "Your legs will never stand it."

"Wait a minute! How come James still does it?"

"James wears knee pads."

What's the difference between a female vocalist and a terrorist?

You can negotiate with a terrorist.

What does a chick singer say when she wakes up in the morning?

"Hey, are you guys all in the same band?"

How do you make a chain saw sound like a heavy metal singer?

Add vibrato.

What was the epitaph on the blues singer's grave?

"I didn't wake up this morning. . . ."

How can you tell when your lead singer is out of tune?

His lips are moving.

"Can you read music?" the producer asked the newly signed lead singer.

"Not enough to hurt my singing."

"I think we might have a problem with that new lead singer," said the bassist to the drummer.

"What makes you think so?"

"Well, half an hour after he left, I went into the bathroom and the mirror was still warm."

How do rock singers usually propose?

"You're *what?!*"

[Shaddapa You Face]

Why should rectal thermometers never be used on singers?

They cause brain damage.

What's the difference between a chick singer and a frog?

They both make the same noise but you can eat the frog's legs.

"On this number," Frank Zappa told his new bassist, "I'd like you to sing solo."

"Really? Wow! I'm flattered."

"Yeah, so low I can't hear you."

How many chick singers does it take to sing "Crazy"?

Apparently all of them.

8

[Have a Laugh on Them]

Jokes about Stars

How does Michael Stipe trash a hotel room?
    He unplugs the TV set.

I'm not saying John Popper's getting a lot fatter, but Rand McNally designed his last record cover.

Pete Townshend took Elton John to see the hot new guitarist from the States when the newcomer played his first U.K. gig in London. The kid played his first song and everybody in the house lit up— he was virtually the new Hendrix. On the second number, he got notes from his guitar and tones out of his amp that no one else had ever dreamed possible. In the midst of the third song, Townshend turned to Elton and said, "Gettin' warm in here, innit, mate?"
    "Not if you're a piano player," Elton replied.

How many Red Hot Chili Peppers does it take to change a light bulb?

One to hold the bulb, one to hold the socket, and the other two to drink till the room spins.

How do you drown Eddie Vedder?

Leave a mirror on the bottom of the swimming pool.

At the Smashing Pumpkins sound check, Billy Corgan spent more than an hour trying to tune his guitar. Finally, the sound guy couldn't stand it any longer and yelled, "Hey, pal, what's taking you so long? Ry Cooder was here just last week, and it only took him two minutes to tune."

To which Billy replied, "See? Some people just don't care."

Did you hear that Silverfish, that new kiddie rock group, broke up?

Their leader got hooked on phonics.

Why does Courtney Love wear panties?

To keep her ankles warm.

Christmas was coming and B. B. King's girlfriend found herself in a quandary. What kind of gift could possibly be appropriate or adequate for the world's greatest blues guitarist? Finally, she had an inspiration and took herself to a tattoo parlor. There she had his initials beautifully etched into her ass—one gorgeous wine-colored *B* on each cheek.

Christmas morning arrived and she rushed downstairs, threw off her clothes, and called, "Oh, B.B., come down and see your Christmas present."

"What you got, girl?"

"No, you must come and see."

"Okay, all right," he said and she heard him walking to the top of the stairs. Quickly, she placed herself at the bottom of the staircase and bent over and grabbed her shins in order to give him the best possible look at the tattoos.

B.B. came down a few steps and halted. "Goddamn, girl, that's really somethin'," he exclaimed. "But who's this guy 'Bob'?"

If Mama Cass had shared that sandwich with Karen Carpenter, they'd both still be singing today.

Eric Clapton and Kirk Hammett of Metallica toured a third world country together. On their day off, they took a walk into the bush, where they were captured by an unfriendly troop of rebel guerillas, who hated the idea of Western culture invading their land. Clapton and Hammett were quickly dragged before a firing squad but, to show that they were not altogether uncivilized, the rebel leader offered each rock star a last request.

"I want to play my guitar one last time," said Hammett.

"Shoot me first," begged Clapton.

Think of Liam Gallagher as the flower of British manhood—a blooming idiot.

What vehicle did the Doors ride around in?
Van Morrison.

What does Kenny G. say when he gets on an elevator?
"Wow! This place rocks!"

When Trent Reznor was a teenager, he begged his dad for guitar lessons. Mr. Reznor, who had been hoping his son would become a concert pianist, finally gave in. After the first lesson, Trent came home very excited.

"Well," asked dad, "how'd the lesson go?"

"It was fantastic! I learned to play two notes on the E string."

"Great! Keep up the good work."

The next week, Trent came home even more excited.

"How was the lesson?" his dad inquired.

"Terrific! Look—I learned to play two notes on the A string."

"Wonderful," said dad. He was impressed despite himself.

The third week, Trent came home several hours late. Mr. Reznor was not amused.

"Young man, *where* have you been? Why are you so late? And why weren't you at your guitar lesson today?"

"Well, it's true I didn't go . . ."

"*Why?* After all your begging and pleading, after all the expense of the guitar, after the money I spent on the amp, after the money I've been giving that guitar teacher . . . now, you not only come home at midnight, you skip the lesson? *What's your excuse, you ungrateful little punk?*"

"I got a gig."

Why did they bury Tupac twenty feet under the ground?

Because deep down he was a swell guy.

Driving to a gig one weekend, Elvis grew bored, so he told his chauffeur to pull over at the next rest stop. They pulled into an obscure corner off the interstate and Elvis decided to take over the wheel. "Sit in the back and enjoy yourself," he told the driver.

Elvis took off but, as usual, he paid no attention to the speed limits. The big, heavy limousine was doing well over eighty when a state trooper pulled him over. The trooper stalked up to the driver's window but as the smoked glass rolled down, and he saw who was sitting at the wheel, he gulped and said, "I have to radio in to headquarters. I'll be right back. Don't go anywhere."

Quickly, he returned to his car and radioed his commanding officer. "Listen, I pulled over somebody *really* important for speeding."

"Who?" asked his captain.

"Well, I'm not sure. But Elvis is his chauffeur."

A friend of ours got an Elvis Presley vibrator for Christmas. It has two speeds: "Love Me Tender" and "All Shook Up."

Chuck Berry goes to jail for tax evasion. Allan Klein goes to jail for tax evasion. What does this mean?

A fool and his money are soon audited.

Willie Nelson, in the midst of a world tour, landed in Sydney, Australia. On the way to the hotel from the airport, he started ranting to his limo driver about the small airport and how in Texas, they have bigger runways on their ranches. Soon they crossed the Sydney Harbor Bridge and Willie started in again: "I have a duck pond bigger than that harbor, and an ornamental bridge that makes this look like a toy!" The Sydney-Newcastle expressway also met with his disdain. "Is this a road or a track?" he sneered. So, when a kangaroo leaped into the middle of the road, causing a near-collision, the limo driver couldn't resist remarking: "Stupid grasshopper!"

We always enjoy a Pink Floyd show, whether we need the sleep or not.

George Michael insisted, during one interview, "I'm not as dumb as I look."
Replied the interviewer: "Who is?"

Steven Tyler's mouth is so big he's thinking about making a duet album with himself.

A couple of days after Buddy Rich died, one of his sidemen called his house and asked the widow if he could talk to Buddy.
"I'm sorry," she said. "But Buddy's dead." The musician apologized and hung up.
The next day, though, he called again and asked the same question.
"I'm sorry," said Mrs. Rich. "Buddy's dead." He said he was sorry, and hung up.
When he called again on the third day, Buddy's wife said, "Look, I talked to you yesterday. I talked to you the day before yesterday. I told you the same thing I'm telling you now: Buddy's dead! Do you understand?"
"Sure, I understand," the musician said. "I just love hearing it."

• • •

On Halloween, Marilyn Manson's parents sent him out as-is.

What's the best way to applaud for Hootie and the Blowfish?
Clap both hands over your ears.

Trent Reznor's so skinny he has to tease his pubic hair to keep his pants up.

Why were Stevie Wonder's hands purple?
He heard it through the grapevine.

Alice Cooper's wife came home early from the country club golf tournament. There stood her teenage son, dressed in bra, panty hose, pearls, and earrings, prancing in front of a mirror. "Son, I don't believe this!" she exclaimed. "We've told you a million times: Stay out of your father's things."

Bruce Springsteen showed up incognito—no earrings.

Then there was the night the Grateful Dead played "When the Swallows Come Back to Capistrano" as an encore. As they left the stage, Jerry Garcia spotted a stranger standing by himself, weeping horribly.
"Gee, are you from Capistrano?" Garcia asked.
"No, I'm a musician."

[Have a Laugh on Them]

Let's see if we get this right: Michael Jackson does everything he can to keep his image in front of us twenty-four hours a day, seven days a week; he wants to be known as the King of Pop and treated as the Master of the Musical Universe. Then he goes to Disneyland and puts on dark glasses and a fake beard so no one will recognize him?

Mariah Carey's singing is mutiny on the high Cs.

Do I believe in reincarnation? You mean, do I believe that Green Day got that obnoxious in just one lifetime?

It's not that Michael Bolton is dull, but we do hear he's started a foundation for yawn research.

"How old is Keith Richards?"
    "Fifty-one."
    "Did you look that up?"
    "No, I counted the rings under his eyes."

It's not true that the guys in Oasis act stupid. It's no act.

Did you hear what happened when Dave Matthews and his band got to the southern tip of Florida?
    It was the first time they'd all ever been in the same key at the same time.

Aerosmith is so popular in New England that Massachusetts named a town after Steven Tyler—Marblehead.

Robbie Robertson, vain? Well, the cops did pick him up parked in Lovers' Lane—by himself.

Those guys in Stone Temple Pilots have more brains in their heads than most of us have in our little fingers.

What do you call ten thousand lesbians with automatic weapons?
Militia Etheridge.

"No, Mick is *not* a snob," his publicist explained. "He really does have Perrier on the knee."

One rock journalist told another, "I've got the worst assignment. I've got to travel with Sting on another one of his boast-to-boast tours!"

Why doesn't Elvis Costello ever talk about his IQ?
It's beneath him.

Is the Horde Tour boring? Well, the ads for this year's version proclaim that the venues sleep twenty thousand.

. . .

Mick Jagger's tongue is so long, when he was a kid he used to lick his envelopes after they'd already gone in the mailbox.

It's not that Tupac led a tough life, but when he heard his road manager went into cardiac arrest, he asked how high they'd set bail.

For years, Billy Idol has carried on one of the greatest love affairs in history. Unassisted.

Mick Jagger goes out drinking and nightclubbing and finally staggers in just after dawn. Jerry Hall greets him at the door with a scowl. "What are you doing coming into our home at this hour of the morning?" she demands.

"All the clubs are closed," Jagger replies.

John Mellencamp is a man of few words. He just keeps repeating them.

David Bowie no longer makes up his face. Now, he has to assemble it.

For years, the Spin Doctors played the bar circuit as unknown failures. Now they're known failures.

A lot of people think that before he joined KISS, Gene Simmons was a teacher. But that's not true. He just spent a lot of years in eighth grade.

Define "mixed emotions."

What happens when your band finally gets its first national tour—opening for Barry Manilow.

.   .   .

When he was a little boy, Johnny Rotten's mother washed his mouth out with soap every time he cursed. It didn't help, though—he just learned to like the taste of soap.

Did you hear Lou Reed got kidnapped?
     But after the killers had been around him for an hour, they sent a ransom note offering to return him for expenses.

We don't mind that Eddie Vedder keeps letting his mind go blank—but don't you think he ought to turn off the sound?

When he was a kid, Bob Dylan used to threaten to run away. His mother would say, "Wait a minute. I'll get my keys so I can drive you."

Did you hear about Bill Wyman's wedding? The bride couldn't get any wedding cake, because she hadn't finished her vegetables.

What happens when you play a Merle Haggard song backwards?
     Your truck gets fixed, your dog gets better, your wife comes home, and they let you out of jail.

. . .

Based on that Moody Blues album, *In Search of the Lost Chord*, it's probably just hiding—in self-defense.

What was the last thing that went through Kurt Cobain's brain?
A bullet.

One thing about Smashing Pumpkins—they didn't let success go to their wardrobe.

Sonny Bono being elected to Congress is proof enough that Lincoln was right: You *can't* fool all of the people, all of the time.
Doing it every couple of years on election day will suffice. (Actually, it's easy to understand how Sonny got elected. If he lived in your town, you'd want him to move far away, too.)

Why do the Ramones' boots have TGIF written on them?
"Toes go in first."

Henry Rollins makes me feel like a bored proctologist—I've seen enough of *that* asshole.

Steven Tyler's mouth is so big, sometimes he whispers in his own ear.

Do you think if we gave Celine Dion a going-away present, she would?

[Have a Laugh on Them]

What were the three happiest years of Ted Nugent's life?

Third grade.

What would it take to reunite the Beatles?

Three more bullets.

What do Michael Jackson and JCPenney have in common?

Both have boys' pants half off.

During a break in the recording session, one of the guitar players went up to the roof to get some air. He heard a noise in the street and leaned over to take a look at what was happening down there. Leaning just a little too far, though, he began to fall. It was six stories to the ground, and he seemed a sure goner. But, just as he was about to hit the pavement with an almighty *splat*, a flatbed truck carrying a load of featherbeds drove by. He hit *plop* in the middle of them, and once the truck stopped at the corner, climbed down, without a scratch.

"Wow!" said one of the band's road crew, who'd witnessed the whole thing and then rushed to the street. "You must be the luckiest musician in the world."

"No," said the guitarist, shaking his head sagely. "That would be Bob Weir."

9

[Know-Nothings and
Know-It-Alls]

Jokes about Critics and Criticism

How many rock critics does it take to change a light bulb?

A thousand. One to change it and 999 to figure out its influences.

Fifty rock critics went to see a dance band. Halfway through the set, they were all moving in different directions. The dance floor looked like a spastics convention. Concerned, the band's manager went over to an editor standing in the corner. "What's going on here?" he asked.

"Oh, they're not dancing to the *music*," the editor explained. "They're dancing to the words."

Did you hear Michael Bolton just finished his last album? At least, all the critics hope so.

The best thing about industrial rock is that, when the record wears out, it still sounds the same.

Then there was the rock star who ran into a critic at the movies. Afterward, they went out for coffee. "I don't get it," the star said. "My records get worse and worse, but they sell more and more."

"Naw," explained the critic. "Your records aren't getting any worse. But you've got more experience now, so your taste is getting better."

Why are rock critics like diapers?
They're always on somebody's butt, and they're usually full of crap.

"Say, did you hear our new album?" the rocker asked the rock critic.
"Yes, but there was a big problem."
"Gee, what was it?"
"I had the volume turned up."

"Hey," said the outraged singer to the rock critic, "my band really didn't deserve what you wrote about us!"
"I know, but I couldn't think of anything worse to say."

What do you get when the staff of *Spin* teams up with Dykes on Bikes?
Even more people who don't do dick.

Kenny G felt despondent over his reviews. So he called the Suicide Hotline, and played them one of his albums. Turning the volume down, he said, "Was that so bad?"

The hotline operator replied, "What are you waiting for?"

"Hey," complained another pop star to the critic, "that review doesn't do me justice!"

"You don't want justice," the critic replied. "You want mercy."

As one rock critic said to the other at the Grateful Dead concert, "Let's all stand and give them a round of ammunition."

"Please tell me what you think of my work. Be honest," the aspiring songwriter asked the notoriously brutal rock critic.

"I believe that your songs will be performed long after Chuck Berry and Bob Dylan have lost their reputation."

"Honest? Wow!"

"Yep, but while people still remember 'em, you'd better get a day job."

10

[Perils of the Biz]

A musician goes out on the road and comes home to find his house burned down to the ground, his family and pets missing. He asks a neighbor what happened.

"Gee, I don't know how to tell you this," his pal tells him, "but while you were gone your manager came to the house, burned it down, raped your wife, kidnapped your kids, and killed your dogs."

"Wait a minute! Wait a minute!" the shocked musician says. "You mean to tell me, my *manager* came to my *house*?"

How many producers does it take to change a light bulb?

Two. One to ask the engineer to do it, and the other to say, "I dunno. What do you think?"

Did you hear about the manager who quit in disgust?

He said he was sick and tired of giving the band eighty-five percent of his money.

The rock singer's wife came in with a brand new fur coat. He immediately flipped out. "We can't afford that."

"But honey, I got it for a song."

"Yeah, well, it better be a hit."

The old-time record mogul was renegotiating with his biggest star. "I've gotta have at least a ten percent royalty," said the star.

"Oh, you can have twelve percent," said the mogul.

"Gee, why, that's very generous."

"Of course, I'm still only gonna *pay* you six percent. But the contract can say whatever you want."

A brief guide to record industry analysis: A hit is when your record comes out and makes the Top Forty. A flop is when your buddy's record comes out and makes the Top Twenty but doesn't make the Top Ten. A hype is when somebody you don't like puts out a record that makes the Top Ten but doesn't get to Number One.

What do you get when you play new age music backwards?

New age music.

The big recording session is about to begin. Everyone is wearing headphones, and right after the engineer says, "Quiet, tape's rolling!" there's a huge drum crash. And from the booth, the producer yells, "All right! Who did that?"

Nobody had seen Barry, the guitar player, for a couple of weeks, so Mitch, the drummer, went over to his house to look for him. He wasn't there, and his wife seemed reluctant to talk about it.

Finally, she said, "Look, he's not here because . . . Well, all you guys in the band are always bragging about your Porsches and your Ferraris, you seem to change cars every few months. But you know, we had kids earlier than the rest of you, and then Barry wasn't *in* the band for the first two tours, so he's never been able to keep up. Finally, the other day, he got so frustrated, he went out and *stole* a Porsche. Naturally, he got caught and now he's going to do three years."

"Gee," said Mitch sympathetically, "that's really awful. But how come Barry couldn't buy one and not make the payments like the rest of us?"

A guy goes into a pet store to buy a songbird. "I want a bird who can sing with the power of Joplin and the grace of Elvis," he said. "It should have the phrasing of Linda Ronstadt and the range of Whitney Houston."

"Fine," said the owner, showing him a lovely golden bird. "This one will cost you five thousand dollars. But there's a catch. You also have to take this one." He pointed to a scraggly brown bird in the cage next door. "He's ten grand."

"Look, the price is fine, but what the hell do I want with both birds? I'll give you fifteen thousand for the golden bird and you can keep the brown one.''

"Won't work," said the owner.

"Why the hell not?"

"The brown bird is the producer."

Then there was the record company geek who decided to invent the microwave CD player, so he could listen to an hour-long album in only six minutes.

"Now the one rule we have to make here," said the record company president, "is that no word of this renegotiation leaks out to our other artists."

"Don't worry," replied the manager, "we're ashamed of how cheap you bastards are, too!"

Why is a concert promoter like sperm?

Each has a one-in-a-million chance of becoming a human being.

What were the sixties like? Back then, your average rock star would charter a plane for $25,000, check into a $500-a-night hotel suite, hire a car for $250 to take him two hundred miles to an ashram, and spend a couple of weeks meditating on how to overcome materialism. Then he'd go home and write an album about how the guru tried to rip him off.

Every industry has its own special language. For instance, when a record company geek wants to say "Screw you," he never resorts to anything that vulgar. He just says, "Trust me."

Then there was the heavy metal star who renegotiated his own $10 million contract. He got ten dollars a year for a million years.

What's the surest way to stop the spread of AIDS?
Let BMG distribute it.

Little Jimmy got sent home from school with a note from the teacher asking his parents to talk to her about a most serious matter. Concerned, they came to school the next morning and were immediately sent into the principal's office. After several minutes' wait, the teacher came in, wearing a perplexed look.

"Yesterday was careers day, and the kids were sharing what their parents did for a living. Finally, Jimmy's turn came and he said, 'My dad is a towel boy in a whorehouse.' Well, I was mortified and the other children got very confused. There was a lot of explaining to do for the rest of the afternoon.

"Now, I certainly don't mind whatever it is you may do for a living, but you shouldn't tell Jimmy that you work in a whorehouse."

"Well, what do you want me to do?" complained the father. "Tell him the truth and admit I work for a record company?"

What's the difference between a schoolteacher and a rock star?
About half a million bucks a year.

"You've got such a famous, crafty manager. How'd he manage to lose all your dough?"
"He was so busy learning the tricks of the trade, he never learned the trade."

•   •   •

[Perils of The Biz]   57

How many A&R men does it take to change a light bulb?

I'll get back to you on that.

What's the difference between a concert promoter and a catfish?

One is a greedy, bottom-feeding scum-sucker. The other is a fish.

Eighty percent of record company geeks were bottle babies. Which proves one thing—even their mothers didn't trust 'em. (And that was *before* they grew teeth.)

My ancestors were taught that the world was flat. At school, they taught me that the world is round. But it wasn't till I took this record company job that I realized it's really crooked.

Define "friend."

In the music world, someone who has the same enemies you do.

Billy and Joe had been struggling with their crummy little band for years. They weren't bad, exactly, just not good enough to get off the bar circuit. Month after month for the better part of a decade, they stumbled from town to town through the Midwest and the Rust Belt, working with an assortment of equally mediocre musicians. They struggled through winter after winter in a van with a heater that nearly asphyxiated them (when it worked) and broke down with increasing regularity, playing in dives so sleazy that even their third-rate booking agent sometimes seemed embarrassed to send them out.

Late one afternoon, as they sat by their stalled vehicle on the outskirts of a small West Virginia town, waiting for a tow, another band drove by. Its brand-new van had the group's logo beautifully painted on the side; the longhairs inside chortled and waved as they drove by. The scent of herb drifted over to the roadside as they sped on.

"Gee, that doesn't look like a bad life," said Billy.

"Aw, I bet they have day jobs," said Joe.

How do you get a record company geek out of a tree?

Cut the rope.

"Hey," said the aspiring singer-songwriter. "Since I made that demo. I've got three companies chasing after me!"

"Really," said his friend, impressed.

"Yep, Visa, MasterCard, and American Express."

How is a record contract like God?

The large print giveth, and the fine print taketh away.

How do you call last year's veejay?

"Hey, cabbie!"

• • •

It was the typical backstage Thanksgiving. The band bitched, the crew gave thanks for what they received (because they were worried about getting what they deserved), the managers huddled in a corner giving thanks for not getting caught, and the promoter was out front, thanking the scalpers while they paid him off.

What is the sweetest sound in the music business? Somebody else's record falling off the charts.

[fanatics on display]

The Fans

What has 100 legs and no pubic hair?
> The front row at a Bon Jovi concert.

What did the Deadhead say when his pot ran out?
> "This band sucks!!"

Why are rock concerts so great?
> Where else can you go and boo millionaires to their faces?

Then there was the night that Bruce Springsteen and the E Street Band got to the false ending of "Born in the USA" and a guy in the third row stood up and screamed, "Oh God, no! He's forgotten his own song!"

"How tough was that heavy metal show the other night?" the promoter asked his chief of security.
> "Not so bad," replied the bouncer. "We were

able to carry out all the wounded during intermission.''

We ordered the Woodstock pay-per-view but we turned off the TV after two hours. With all the mud in that slam-dancing pit, it was too hard to tell which side was winning.

What is a fan club?
    A group of kids who tell a star he's not alone in his estimation of his own importance.

The woman sat alone at the sold-out Springsteen concert. Dressed in black from head to foot, strikingly attractive, but with an empty seat beside her.
    ''Pardon me, ma'am, but is this seat taken?'' asked an usher.
    ''Well, it's my husband's,'' she replied.
    ''Where is he?''
    ''He died.''
    ''I'm sorry. But couldn't you have given the other ticket to a family member or one of your friends?''
    ''No, they're all at the funeral.''

Define ''gross stupidity.''
    One hundred forty-four fans at Woodstock.

At a folk club, we were seated behind a couple who yakked all through the opening act. Finally, my pal said, ''Look, folks, we can't hear a damn thing!''
    ''We weren't talking to you,'' replied the guy.

About eight-thirty one evening, an old lady comes up to a hippie on Haight Street and asks, "Crosstown buses run all night?"

"Doo dah, doo dah," he replies.

Why does everyone at a Springsteen concert wear T-shirts, sneakers, and jeans?

To express their individuality.

Did you hear about the world's loneliest rock fan?

He joined the Columbia Record Club to meet people at the dances.

"How'd you like the show, son?"

"It was fantastic, Mom. You would have hated it."

What's the difference between a groupie and a washing machine?

A washing machine doesn't follow you around after you dump a load in it.

How many Deadheads does it take to change a light bulb?

None. They just watch it burn out, then follow it around for twenty years.

How can you tell if a Deadhead was crashing at your house?

He's still there.

What do you say to a Deadhead in a three-piece suit?

"Will the defendant please rise?"

 [Fanatics on Display]

I 2

[Hip-Hop on the Drop]

Rap Jokes

Boy, those rap records sell like wildfire—*every-body's* burning them!

Did you hear about the rap group that bought a bird and taught it how to talk? They got arrested for contributing to the delinquency of a mynah.

Cypress Hill got almost a million names on those petitions to legalize pot.

Unfortunately, they kept leaving the gigs and forgetting them.

Ice T just moved into a really nice new house in one of Hollywood's most expensive neighborhoods—and almost died in a drive-by by the Welcome Wagon.

It's not true that 2 Live Crew runs around with prostitutes. They're all volunteers.

Snoop Dogg's brother wanted to start a funeral home, so he had his crew shoot a couple guys to get him started.

In KRS-One's old neighborhood, the most common form of transportation was a stretcher.

We went to a big rap festival last summer with the usual audience—two thousand kids and twenty thousand cops.

2 Live Crew had to fire their road manager. He couldn't keep his mind in the gutter.

[Hip-Hop on the Drop]

Did you hear about the new rap club? They frisk you at the door and if you don't have a gun, they loan you one.

What do you mean rap groups aren't responsible to the youth of their communities? Why, down in Houston, the Geto Boys opened up a gun shop and immediately held a back-to-school sale.

What's got a thousand teeth and holds back a monster?
   Dr. Dre's zipper.

13

[Bar Wars]

What's the bar band musician's salute?

Raise your hand in the air . . . and check your watch.

A bar band musician was told by his doctor that he had a rare degenerative disease, which left him with only one year to live.

"A whole year!" he moaned. "What am I going to live on for a whole year?"

It was another dumb lounge gig in Jersey. The pianist, trying to make it through the last set without falling asleep, noticed a couple of guys walk in and sit down at a ringside table. They were right out of Central Casting for *The Godfather, Part VII*—pinkie rings, sharkskin suits, lacquered hair.

After sitting through "Feelings" and "Love Story," the one who was obviously the sidekick walked over to the piano and stuffed a twenty-dollar bill in the tip jar.

"Hey, mac, da boss wants ya to play 'Strangers in Da Night' in three-four time."

"I'm sorry, sir, but that's totally inappropriate," replied the pianist. After all, even a lounge hack has *some* standards.

The henchman went back to his table. After a quick whispered conference, he returned, this time striding more purposefully.

"Listen, mac, if ya know what's good for ya, you'll play 'Strangers in the Night' in three-four time."

"Listen, you muscle-bound jerk. I hate this job. And I'm *certainly* not gonna do anything as ridiculous as playing 'Strangers in the Night' in three-four time."

The button man went back to see his Don, and this time, the conference grew much more agitated. When he came back this time, the sidekick was not only practically talking through gritted teeth; he had opened his jacket so the holster could be seen . . . and reached more easily.

"If you don't want every one of yer precious piano-playin' fingers busted right here on the spot, you *will* play 'Strangers in the Night' in three-four time. Do we understand each other?"

"All right, all right. I'll play the goddamn thing, even though it's the most ridiculous piece of music I've ever tried to put over in my life. I'll do it. Just sit down and order your drinks and leave me alone."

The mobster sits down next to his boss, and the pianist reluctantly launches into his request. Suddenly he hears the Don singing along:

"Strangers in the fuckin' night . . ."

How does a lounge musician take a bubble bath?
He eats beans for dinner.

[Bar Wars]   69

How can you tell if a bar band musician is sexually excited?

He's breathing.

How can you tell if a bar band musician is happy?
Who cares?

What is a musician's idea of safe sex?
A padded headboard.

Why were musicians given larger brains than dogs?

So they won't hump women's legs at parties.

Only a bar band musician would buy a five-hundred-dollar car and put a four-thousand-dollar stereo in it.

Overheard backstage: Guitar player to chick singer: "I don't know why you bother wearing a bra. You've got nothing to put in it."

Chick singer: "You wear briefs, don't you?"

A bar owner is auditioning pianists, and it's the very last guy's turn to play. The club owner isn't expecting much. All the other people who'd auditioned were either rank amateurs or utter hacks. But this one plays a nice ballad. "Wow, what a *great* tune. Is it by you? What's it called?"

"Yeah, it's mine. It's called 'Spread Your Legs, You Bitch.' "

"*Whaaat?* Such a nice ballad can't possibly be titled that!"

"Well, that's what I called it."

"Oh, my God," the bar owner mutters to himself. "Err . . . can you play something else?"

"Yep, sure . . . a-one, a-two . . ."

"Whoa, that one's great too. Yeah, it sounds great . . . er . . . what's the title?"

"It's called 'I Want to Wank on Your Boobs.' "

By this time, the poor bar owner is totally confused; the music's great but if the piano player opens his mouth, he's likely to lose all his business and for that matter, maybe even his liquor license. But the music's *so* good, he can't resist. "Well, forget it. I'll hire you, 'cause you do sound great, but you gotta *swear* to God that you won't be saying a single word about anything. You're not even introducing your tunes. Okay?"

"That's fine with me. It's a deal."

That very first night, he's playing and everything is working fine. Then comes the break, and the pianist goes to the bathroom. He finishes, and while leaving, he comes across one of the customers who tells him, "You know, your fly's open, and your cock is showing."

"What do you mean do I know it?! I wrote it!"

14

Backstage and on the Road

Rock 'n' roll tours are held together by three things—gaffer tape, false promises, and zippers. In that order.

What's the difference between a tour manager and a toilet seat?
    The toilet seat only has to deal with one asshole at a time.

What's the difference between a homeless guy and a roadie?
    An all-access laminate.

One band's travel agent called up a hotel chain and asked, "Do you take rock groups?" They replied, "No, only cash and credit cards."

· · ·

Steve, the band's new accountant, kept pretty quiet about it but in private life, he practiced Christianity quite devoutly. Though he avoided most occasions of sin, he nevertheless managed to conduct himself as one of the gang whenever the crew came around to collect their pay and expense money. But he did wear a small golden cross around his neck.

One day, Mike learned that the accountant was a Christian. "Did you know that Steve was religious?" he asked Doug.

"Of course," said Doug. "He's a certified accountant. That's why he gets to wear that plus sign around his neck."

How do you break a roadie's finger?
    Smack him in the nose.

What's the mating call of the road crew?
    "I'm sooooo drunk!"

How do you keep the road crew busy on its day off?
    Give them each a pack of M&Ms and make them alphabetize them.

On a tour of Italy, the band checked into the country's fanciest hotel, making themselves comfortable in the posh digs for several days before the show. The concert went great and they went back to get some rest. Near dawn, however, the office suite was invaded by a pair of masked bandits carrying sawed-off shotguns. They cornered the tour manager and the production coordinator and demanded the show receipts. Unfortunately, only the production coordinator spoke Italian, while only the tour manager knew where the money was hidden.

At first, the roadies tried to tough it out. The bandit leader immediately responded with a long, sharp statement in Italian. "What'd he say?" the tour manager asked breathlessly.

"He said that if we don't tell him where the money is, they're going to kill you."

"Well, I don't wanna die for somebody else's dough. Tell him that the money is hidden in a secret compartment in my suitcase in the other room."

So the production manager turned to the bandits and said in Italian, "He says he'd rather die with honor than give up the cash."

How many roadies does it take to change a light bulb?

One, but he has to use an entire roll of gaffer tape.

How many California roadies does it take to change a light bulb?

Three—the guy with the gaffer tape does the work and the other two share the experience.

How many New York roadies does it take to change a light bulb?

Fuck off! And gimme that gaffer tape back!

Mike and Doug, the moronic roadies, stood backstage playing with their expensive new Maglite flashlights—the kind stage crews use to lead musicians onstage in the dark with a pencil-thin beam. Suddenly, Mike discovered that if you twisted the lens, a much broader beam could also be projected. He aimed it at the ceiling, and said to Doug, "I dare you to climb that beam all the way to the rigging."

"Oh, no, you don't," said Doug. "I know you—I'll get halfway up and you'll turn off the flashlight!"

How many lighting designers does it take to change a light bulb?

Who cares?

The roadies had just come off a tour with an all-female band. They'd traveled by bus. "Where did you stop?" their pal back home asked.

"At every rest station."

What's the most common thing roadies do with their assholes?

Set up their equipment.

Doug and Mike were putting up the stage. Doug had a hammer and was attempting to nail together a couple of boards, but he held the nail with the pointed end facing the hammer, flat end facing the board.

"Hey!" said Mike, "you're doing that wrong. That nail's for the other side."

.   .   .   🐷

Why do roadies chew tobacco?
    To sweeten their breath.

What's a seven course meal to a roadie?
    A hot dog and a six-pack.

How many roadies does it take to make a batch of chocolate chip cookies?
    Five. One to mix the dough, four to peel the M&Ms.

How many roadies does it take to make popcorn?
    Three. One to hold the pan, two to shake the stove.

Two well-aged roadies are talking. "I've been out with the Who, Aerosmith, the Clash, some of the loudest bands in the world. And it hasn't affected my hearing a damn bit," says the first one. "Why, I can even hear my watch ticking."

    "You've got a digital watch. Are you sure it ticks?" says his friend.

    "Eleven-thirty," says the first burnout.

The two roadies had been engaged in a hot debate about politics throughout the overnight bus trip. Finally, as dawn broke, they dozed off and silence reigned. But only briefly. "Jesus!" said the guitar player, "what intellectual combat!"

    "Yeah," said the cynical bassist. "Fortunately, both of them were unarmed."

•   •   •

"I've worked for this band for twenty years of practices, and I've never heard them raise their voices to one another."

"Were you already deaf when they hired you?"

"Do you have any references?" the tour manager asked the aspiring roadie.

"I've worked for more than a dozen bands," he replied.

"Really. How long have you been doing this?"

"Eight months."

Doug and Mike had to travel on the bus from their hotel for a half hour before they got to the new suburban arena. "Jesus!" Doug complained. "Why the hell did they put this place all the way out here?"

"Stupid!" said Mike. "This is where everyone comes for the shows."

"How were things out on the road?"

"Awful. The hours sucked, the hotels were terrible, the food backstage was either overcooked or half rotted if it was supposed to be fresh, the bus stank and the heater broke, the band were the biggest bunch of asshole prima donnas I've ever worked with, and the rest of the crew are the biggest bunch of junkies and jackoffs you've ever smelled in your life. The bottom of the barrel, man."

"So you quit?"

"Hell, no. It's the first time getting home ever looked so good."

Why is it so hard for a roadie to get into a groupie's pants?

They already have an asshole there.

The new roadie stood backstage while the band took their places. "All right," the production manager said. "Everybody's ready. Run up the curtain."

"What the hell do you think I am?" asked the roadie. "A squirrel?"

What do a shoe store and backstage have in common?

A couple hundred loafers.

Why do the stagehands always clap for an encore?

Because they get time and a half for overtime.

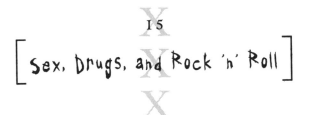

15

[Sex, Drugs, and Rock 'n' Roll]

The backstage argument concerned sex. The rock star argued that sex was sixty percent work and forty percent fun. No, said his manager, sex is about eighty percent work and twenty percent fun. Finally, they decided to ask a roadie.

"Sex is a hundred percent work, and it isn't any fun at all," the roadie told them.

"Huh? How do you figure?" asked the star.

"Well, if it were any fun, you'd keep it all for yourself."

If good little girls go to heaven, where do bad little girls go?

Backstage.

"Man, you're really drinking a lot lately," says the lead guitarist to his band's bass player.

"Yeah, I know," said the bassist. "But if I do enough of it, it makes it harder to see the pimples."

"You don't have pimples."

"No, but all those girls backstage do."

"Our new bassist is so cute!" complained the backup singer. "But he has such awful dandruff . . ."

"Have you tried offering him Head and Shoulders?"

"No. I didn't know you could give shoulders."

After the show, the road manager led no less than six beautiful women into the star's dressing room. "Wow!" a record company geek asked, "what's he going to do with all *that?*"

"Oh it's basically rock 'n' roll roulette," explained the road manager. "He gets to spend the night with any one of them—all of them will let him do whatever he wants, but one of them is writing a book and will sue his ass off."

What's the difference between a light bulb and a groupie with HIV?

You can *un*screw a light bulb.

Terribly concerned about how his album recording project was coming along, the star couldn't sleep, could barely eat, lashed into the wife and kids, and refused to communicate with his producer, musicians, and engineers except in the most cryptic grunts and moans. Finally, his manager convinced him to seek out a psychiatrist. "Look, this can't be resolved just by talking. I recommend that you take Prozac every day. Then we'll get together and talk things over next week."

A week later the star showed up at the

shrink's office. "How's the record coming along?" asked the doc.

"Who cares?" answered the star.

Rock 'n' roll is like sex—you don't have to be good at it to have fun.

Why does Tipper Gore hate premarital sex?
    It sometimes leads to dancing.

On his wedding night, Bob was amazed to find that his new bride was an adept and experienced lover. "Say," he said, when he'd caught his breath. "I thought you told me you'd only had sex once before."

    "That's true."

    "Well, who were you with?"

    "The Rolling Stones."

It had been the best year of the star's career. His new album had sold more than ten million copies; his video won every MTV award; his first movie came out and did big box office, while the sound track sold another five million; and his worldwide concert tour had sold out houses on every continent except Antarctica.

    When he returned home to L.A., his manager had arranged to have his home totally renovated. It now featured beautifully furnished living quarters, a screening room, a full-scale 48-track recording studio with live-in engineer, stables and kennels, quarters for servants and guest musicians, and a huge billiard room. But the star didn't really get excited till they got to the new pool, Olympic-sized and perfectly landscaped. Hanging around it were several beautiful young women from the neighborhood, sunning themselves or sporting in the water.

The star stopped and stared. "Gee, Rod," the manager said nervously, "I hope you don't mind . . ."

"No, no, I love the pool. It's just that I didn't imagine that you'd already have it *stocked*."

It had been one hell of a tour. A virtual orgy in every town for six months. The singer arrived home sated but when he got up the morning after, his daydreams turned to nightmare. He had a bright red rash all around his groin. Terrified, he called his manager who made an appointment with a specialist, who shook his head sadly, and referred him to a second doctor. But that doctor referred him to a third, and then a fourth.

Finally, he went to see the same general practitioner he'd been seeing since youth. The star sat on the edge of the examining table close to tears while the doctor looked at him from the doorway. "Okay, pull 'em back up, go home, and give it a good wash. On the way out, give the receptionist fifty bucks."

"But the other doctors charged a lot of money and didn't know what the hell was going on."

"Yeah, well, maybe they don't know as much about lipstick as I do."

What's the first thing a groupie does in the morning?

Gets dressed and hurries off to the school bus.

16

[The Final Chapter]

Life after Rock 'n' Roll

A famous rock star dies and the next morning, his record company immediately convenes a marketing meeting. The executives and bureaucrats assemble wearing long faces, in shock from the death of such a celebrated figure. They even begin the discussion by tossing around the idea of issuing no new records for a year, out of respect for the dead. But the president of the company points out that the fans will want a memento of their hero, that the artist's family deserves a fitting memorial and . . .

"Let's face it, guys," the company's marketing director cuts in, "he's only gonna die *once*."

Three guys are in the lobby of heaven, waiting to see if they'll be admitted. St. Peter calls the first one over, and says, "Tell me about your life."

"Well, I made some mistakes, but basically, I believe I lived the life of a good man. My wife and I raised two great kids, and we went to church occasionally."

"Who cares?" St. Peter yawns. "How much money did you make?"

"Oh, I was a very successful doctor. I guess I made a couple million over the years."

"Okay, you're in!"

The second guy walks over and says, "Look, I have to admit I wasn't a very good man. I lied and cheated. I married my third wife before the second divorce was final, I ripped off my business associates, and by the end, my kids wouldn't speak to me. But at the end of my life, I . . ."

"Who cares?" St. Peter says. "How much *money* did you make?"

"Oh, I was a commodities broker, so I made probably thirty million bucks."

"Well, come on in!"

By now, the third guy is getting pretty nervous. Trembling, he walks up to St. Peter and starts telling him about all his charity work, the time he spent volunteering at a homeless shelter, taking care of his ill and aged parents.

St. Peter cuts him off: "Hey, are you paying attention here? *I don't care* about any of that. How much *money* did you make—lifetime?"

"Well, okay," the guy says with a sigh. "In my entire life, I made $18,754.93."

"Hey man," says St. Peter, "what do you play?"

A rock critic died and went to heaven. (That's not the joke.) When he got there, he found to his amazement that music and great musicians were absolutely everywhere. A friend from a record label guided him around, showing him Kurt Cobain's cloud, the place where Jimi Hendrix held his month-long jam sessions, Janis Joplin's blues bar, and all the other sights.

[The Final Chapter]

Suddenly, the newcomer pulled his friend aside. "Hey, what's going on here? I only died the other day, and everyone in U2 was all still alive. What's Bono doing over there?"

"Oh, that's not Bono," his pal replied. "That's God. He just *thinks* he's Bono."

When Kurt Cobain died, he found himself in a strange place. He couldn't figure out for sure whether he was in heaven or whether it was hell. He walked strange empty corridors for a while, when suddenly he spotted Elvis.

Quickly, Cobain ducked around the corner, muttering to himself, "Shit, this *must* be hell."

Meanwhile, Elvis mumbled to himself, "Gawd-*damn!* I can't believe they let punks in up here!"

A musician died and went to heaven, where he met an old bandmate. He asked what the scene up there was like.

"Hey man, it's incredible. Every day, there's this jam with all the greats: Jimi Hendrix, Keith Moon, Buddy Holly, Frank Zappa, all those guys. You can sit in and you *always* sound great! There's only one problem."

"Hey, this is heaven! How could there be a problem?"

"God has a girlfriend, and she likes to sing."

Elvis died and got to the heavenly gates. St. Peter greeted him effusively, although he didn't know him from Adam. "What did you do during your lifetime?" asked the saint.

"Well, they called me the King of Rock 'n' Roll," said Elvis.

"Then you certainly can't stay here," replied the holy gatekeeper.

"Gawd-damn! You mean, I died and I *still* gotta stay on RCA?" Elvis moaned.

The aging rock star lay on his death bed, wasted from a life of complete dissolution: Girls, boys, drugs, drink, staying up all night, bouncing around the world. Very few people had come to visit him during his final illness, because he had treated so many so shabbily and with such great arrogance over the years. But his brother, the preacher, did come to attend to him in his final crisis.

"Steven, you must repent," his brother insisted. "You must renounce the devil and all his works. You must accept Christ, and with the life you've led, you must reject Satan!"

"I'm sorry," said his brother, "but I just can't do that. Where I'm headed, it's best not to make those kinds of enemies."

The Pope died, and of course he went to heaven. St. Peter was showing him around, and took him to his new neighborhood, which he shared with Gandhi, Buddha, and Moses. All of the religious men had similar quarters: well-appointed bungalows on a quiet hillside. On top of the hill, however, was a beautiful mansion.

"Excuse me," asked the Pope, "but whose house is that?"

"Duke Ellington's," answered St. Peter.

"*What!* Do you mean to tell me that the Pope gets a bungalow and Duke Ellington, a mere musician, gets a mansion? I was a pious man and a great religious leader—he played *jazz!*"

"Well, Your Holiness, that's just the point," St. Peter replied. "Around here, religious men are a dime a dozen. But there's only one jazz musician."

Frank Zappa had just finished his first week of the afterlife. Surprised that there even was one, he hadn't really had time to stop and consider all the implications. But that afternoon, he did ask Lester Bangs, "Hey, you know, I've met all sorts of famous rock stars here, and even a few pop singers. How come I haven't met any classical musicians?"

"Oh, you know that wall of clouds that looks like a fence? Well, the classical guys are all on the other side," the rock critic explained. "They think they're the only ones here."

When Miles Davis died, he found himself confronting both St. Peter and the Devil. They informed him that he had a rare opportunity to choose between heaven and hell. Miles asked if he could have a look at each place before making his choice.

"Of course," they replied, "but once you choose, the decision's final."

St. Peter took Davis on a tour of heaven, where he saw sunny meadows, lovely scenery, and a lot of drippy-looking squares sitting around playing harps. After a few minutes, he begged for the chance to check out hell.

The Devil led him to a smokey club where Count Basie led a band with Monk on piano, Dizzy on trumpet, Coltrane on sax, and a host of other jazz greats waiting in the wings for their turn to blow.

"This is it for me!" Miles exclaimed. Instantly, he was thrown into a vat of burning oil while demons prodded him with pitchforks.

"Hey! What's going on?" he screamed.

A sly grin slowly spread across the Devil's face. "Nice demo, huh?"

The two bandmates had played together for more than ten years, and considered themselves best friends. They made a pact that, whichever one died first, he'd come back and tell his buddy about the afterlife. Sure enough, after one of them was shot during a barroom brawl, he returned to give his pal the 411.

"I've got some good news and some bad news," he said. "The good news is that there really is a rock 'n' roll heaven. There's a gig every night, the PA's great, the roadies know what they're doing, the catering's edible . . . there's even enough towels in the dressing room."

"So what's the bad news?"

"You're headlining tomorrow."

If it's heaven, why do the angels play harps?

Oh yeah. . . .
Best joke of all: The Rock and Roll Hall of Fame is located in Cleveland.